THE DARK TAKES AIM

THE DARK TAKES AIM

poems by Julie Suk

Autumn House Press

"Autumn House" and "Autumn House Press" are registered trademarks owned by Autumn House Press, a non-profit corporation whose mission is the publication and promotion of poetry.

Text and cover design: Kathy Boykowycz
Editorial Consultant: Eva Maria Simms
Marketing Consultant: Michael Wurster
Cover: sculpture by Russ Thayer, used by permission

Printed in the USA
Library of Congress Control Number: 2003110473
ISBN: 0966941985

"It is possible that there is no other memory than the memory of wounds."
Czeslaw Milosz

The Autumn House Poetry Series
Michael Simms, editor

OneOnOne by Jack Myers
Snow White Horses, Selected Poems 1973-1988
  by Ed Ochester
The Leaving, New and Selected Poems
  by Sue Ellen Thompson
Dirt by Jo McDougall
Fire in the Orchard by Gary Margolis
Just Once, New and Previous Poems by Samuel Hazo
The White Calf Kicks by Deborah Slicer
  (2003 Autumn House Poetry Prize, selected by
  Naomi Shihab Nye)
The Divine Salt by Peter Blair
The Dark Takes Aim by Julie Suk

For Dannye, Dede, Lucinda, Mary Hunter and Susan

CONTENTS

DEMOLITIONS

DRAWN INTO ARMS

HAUNTED BY RUIN

Publication of this book is made possible by a grant from The Pittsburgh Foundation.

Additional support has been provided by The International Poetry Forum.

ACKNOWLEDGMENTS

Grateful acknowledgment is made to the editors of the following journals in which these poems first appeared, some in slightly different versions: *American Literary Review*: "Paradise with Basso Continuo"; *The Broad River Review*: "A Troubled Sky" and "Rainbow Falls"; *The Chariton Review*: "The Architecture of Ruin" and "Cézanne's Apples"; *Chelsea*: "Bound as I Am," "Loving the Hands" and "Reeling into Night"; *Connecticut Review*: "Burials" and "Running Away"; *Cream City Review*: "Listening to Rodrigo's Concerto for Guitar"; *Great River Review*: "In Praise Of The Living," "Within the Frame"; *The Laurel Review*: "Divorce"; *Poetry*: "The Acres You Cross," "From Ruin," "Haunted by Ruin," "Lamentation," "Leaving the World We've Loved Speechless," "Rounds" and "Today You Traverse the Mountain"; *The Review, McNeese State*: "From The Water Meadows"; *Shenandoah*: "Where We Are" and "Yesterday"; *Sycamore Review*: "Stalking"; *Tar River Poetry*: "Fracture," "Lie Down with Me," "Open to Change" and "Taking Back the Given."

"Leaving the World We've Loved Speechless" appeared in *And What Rough Beast: Poems at the End of the Century*, edited by Robert McGovern and Stephen Haven; The Ashland Poetry Press, 1999. "Today You Traverse the Mountain" appeared in *No Hiding Place: Uncovering the Legacy of Charlotte-Area Writers*, edited by Frye Gaillard, Amy Rogers and Robert Inman; Down Home Press, 1999. "From Ruin" appeared in *The POETRY Anthology 1912-2002*, edited by Stephen Young and Joseph Parisi; The Modern Poetry Association, 2002.

DEMOLITIONS

At a distance:
seemingly intact piers,
dark recesses, blind arcades.

Nearer, the sky
pours through arches,
a drizzle of rain inside the nave,
the passage crumbling,
open to grass and grazing sheep.

On good days
strokes of sun the trespasser,
devastation given a kind of splendor,

the strobe lights of memory
playing out impressions of a tower
you know is not there,

nor are the bells,
nor the stalls, nor choir,
not one finger tapping time
on the carved arms of chairs
or intertwined

here the church,
here the steeple,
open the door

no vaulting hosannas, the chalice
and wine of remembrance
long removed,

as were the tapestries,
as was the incense of flesh
not yet carrion, not yet stringing off
into sorrow, base silence.

Three a.m., the house a foreign country I wake in,
same language but a different inflection,
a creak on the stair a harbinger,
this jolt into insomnia an alert.

In an etching by Goya, demons perch on a bedpost
and clamor for the sleeper's heart.

Long ago we knelt for prayers
but those children have slept for years,
dreams merging, child into beast.
                     Somewhere
a truck explodes and bodies bloom
with the fleshy extravagance of peonies—
                   forgive me,
not petals but a scream settling on entrails,
bone, meat, our betrayals piling in gutters.

It should be obvious where the fault lies,
yet we continue to build there, the structure
collapsing into itself, the century in ruins.
                     Somewhere
a trail remains, linking our inlands,
the path to summers in the mountains
where a halo of hummingbirds
crowns the feeder,
rock hectored by a snow-fed river,
mist from the falls beading our hair.

Moving as we do from the body
and its parochial demands to lessons of love,
you might say we succeed as often as not,
on call even as we sleep.
                   Even as we sleep,
the cry of a puma cracks the night.

When I held my first son,
how perfect he seemed.
Driving home late,
we would sing rounds
O how lovely is the evening
his head nodding to my lap.

Blessings on that third
of our lives spent in sleep,
the plots of the day
left dangling.

Once I drove by a woman
clinging to a viaduct's ledge,
police, priest, and the curious
crowded below, the road
curving past into a benign
vista of cows and trees.

Blessings on those moments of reprieve
grabbed before dropping into nightmare.

How could my son fracture,
unaware of the split?
Ominous, the day I waited
on his porch, cake in hand
as if food could assuage
a mind reeling off.

Get out! Get out! The door slammed.
What I dread is a stand-off,
barricades, guns, police
with no choice but to shoot.

Blessings on the daughter
who ripens with a life
that turns us around again,
this time, we hope,
the helix of notes
descending in tune.

For a while we let pass
what Aeschylus said,
how at night
the pain that can't forget
falls drop by drop
upon the heart.

The moon floats off,
the dog whimpers under the steps.
How lovely the evening
with a child on my lap,
a circle of us singing
heedless of the dark taking aim.

The keys on a hook by the door,
a copy made for those who are close
and careful with loss.

After tearing up the world
I'm still looking for my glasses.

Would you please remove the clip from your gun.

Let the child's limbs fly back into shape,
torn flesh mending itself.

Leave coffins stacked where they were under dust.
In the market place, let mourners bargain for spice.

The wailing you can't hear is the sorrow I've hidden,
what or who it was I wanted, lost

because I waited too long,
hunger and need shrugged off.

Listen, you say, holding my arms, *listen.*

YESTERDAY

What we knew we didn't know,
recalling only the threat of ice,
a hint of rain, or a dip
in the pool of desire.

As in childbirth, there was pain,
pain that no longer pounds
as it did yesterday,
blood drying under blood.

God gives us only what we can bear.
Is that so? whisper the dismembered,
their bones unable to stroke
the body to a shimmer.

In Siberia, a woman still fleshed
is lifted frozen from a crypt,
her limbs tattooed with a menagerie
of exotic beasts, whorls
of brilliant blue. One of her long
tapered fingers is pointing
as if to touch.

From the headdress and adornments—
probably a priestess. Holy,
the way she is carried
overhead on a canvas bier
to the plane, to the lab
where her body will be plundered.

Such probes leave us wanting,
tell us little
of those who broke away,
now scattered who knows where,
beautiful fragments
we may never recover.

LISTENING TO RODRIGO'S
CONCERTO FOR GUITAR

We've heard the story:
his young wife bleeds
for the child born dead.
Sitting out the night
he leans into the lament,
left foot propped,
legs spread
under the guitar in his arms.
The woman kneels
in that shadowy space
between, his hand
stroking the dark plunge
of hair to breasts,
his hand swooning
over the chords,
one finger pressed there,
another here, probing
the body's thrum,
the audience a held
breath away.
Lay a hand over the heart
and feel it pump, a flow
tuned to the airs of love,
those ways we die.
The woman moans. Shhh,
he strums her to life,
but too much blood has spilled.
The gut contracts
and love goes
taking with it flesh.

IN AND OUT OF RANGE

The weather's sharp today,
blueberries hanging over the trail,
the gyre of a hawk
around the pinnacle.

A few necessities bear us
into the untouched terrain,
our first fires
low and unobtrusive.

Ahead of us a city
reeking with the dead,
the enemy here
crouched under our skin.

*

At night we hide in a cave,
the animals sketched on stone
still admissible,
the outlined hands
filled with our own.

In the corridors, vivid dreams,
variations that repeat
until we give them names.

These are the children
whose arms we load with flowers
sometimes tooled into weapons
they turn on us and aim.

*

My hands are all over you
fingering
what I should know by rote.

I stroke your face,
you pull me close.
This is all I need,
I tell myself,
and for a while disbelieve

the source of everything
we give tongue to
is reduced to a whisper.

And we are not listening.
Echos beat themselves senseless.

Our small lamps barely light
the labyrinth.

FROM RUIN

Our guide is Turk-proud
though he moved from Bosnia as a child.
During the winter he's an archaeology student
on a dig at Tyre—his dig, he smiles.

This morning, newspapers proclaim
the find of another Bosnian grave,
a scramble of the unidentified.

I ask if he has a picture of his girl.
Not with him, he says, and tells us goodbye.
He'll meet her later and drive
through the night to his home in Ankara.
For him there is only one day of rest
before another tour begins.

Pull over and sleep, I advise.

In the desolate steppes ahead,
they'll lie beneath a spread of stars,
only an occasional passing car,
miles of wheat swooning on all sides—

a long whisper across the land,
the promise of grains hanging on,
feeding them for a time,
their bodies close as flesh can get,
the heart, that bloody artifact,
more difficult to find.

I wake to an owl screech,
black feathers scattered,
crows caterwauling around the oak,
one squawking for its lost mate.

My call came at three,
a nightmare crashing through,
your body already cool,
the tick of a fan the only hint
air once stirred with your breath.

Day took over, blazing as it did
on the wheatfield where Van Gogh
shot himself, dying later
cradled in his brother's arms.

The way I held you
in a landscape I can't scumble over,

like the canvas
lashed with cobalt, ocher, black,
the one road dropped by the horizon,
the sky ominous, embittered by crows.

LIE DOWN WITH ME

Lie down with me,
you whispered, and I did
there in the darkness
of your dying, our hands
awkward holding on.

The truth is
I wanted to turn away
from even that small act,
wanted you flushed and whole,
not your sour flesh
no longer firm in my arms.

Silence was how we dealt
with our differences,
knowing a break can happen
before a fall,
the way old people crack
where they stand,
their landing a mere
compound of fracture.

There are nights
memory drifts down
invading hollows and crevices,
a caress so insistent
my body throbs.

After your death I wandered
from country to ruined country.
Once in Konya I woke to hear
a muezzin singing prayers,
the bent notes widening
a vacancy I can't fill.

In the market places, in alleys,
in crumbled alcoves—children
seemed never to sleep.
At night they squatted
by a restaurant door,
and I'd find them there
when I left.

Buy, they begged, and if I said no,
they insisted *Maybe tomorrow,*
please.
Remember me.
Remember my name.

THE DAY

pillaged on its way out
bells diminishing

an urgent note crumpled on a desk

the sun dragging its dusty train
across the threshold

a fragment of color caught
when the latch clicks

In late afternoon clouds flatten out
so that it seems we're sailing into islands and coral seas.

Small cays, dissolving shores,
you and I island-hopping to find the coves we lost track of.

If it were possible to turn back
and start again, would we be blind as before

still subject to the tides
that set us adrift as we waxed and waned?

As a child I let myself go and floated rollers
until I was beached, sea-wash leaching a trough around my body

as if there were no undertow
to pull me beyond reprieve, as if I could escape

to play with flotsam left by the sea—wreckage
covered with oil, u-boats prowling closer than we dreamed.

Lucky for a time,
but coming up fast a towering cumulus
bulges with storms, sooner than later volatile, firing wild.

Half asleep, my husband flails
at a recurrent nightmare—
our son chasing him with a gun.

Careful,
how we step around him.
Any moment he might explode.

I'm dying dying! every illness he can dream
except for the one trapped in his brain,
commitment his greatest fear,

his days split from the long night
he'd like to escape, each settling board
a menacing sound creeping up to do harm.

He twists in a snarl
of messages and intricate plots.

I'm plagued too by night thoughts
and wake wondering how they slip
in and out, graying off
before I can hold them down.

What's the use of this?
my son complains of anything I offer.

His cool stare wary—
a sweetness turned sour.
Nothing I can straighten or comb.
Nothing I can soothe.

When you stand on the bridge
as we did
breathing the acrid scent
of galax and laurel
the day sunny
as it was
spray misting our hair and clothes
you can see a rainbow.

Upstream, swimmers zig-zag
down a rock slope and leap into a pool.
Swim at your own risk, the sign says,
water narrowing between boulders
and surging on to the falls.

Like the roil of days
we dare throw ourselves in, the rush
we crave before pulled out.

No, we don't rope the top,
the ranger explains,
it might encourage more fools,

It was her day off.
Cheerful, a sweet smile, say friends.
She'd do anything for you.

Handed her a limb, the boyfriend sobs,
but she tumbled too fast,
couldn't grab hold.

Clawing the edge, water tearing at her clothes,
rinsing her mouth of screams.

DIVORCE

A tornado rips
the skin off a town.

In the aftermath
silence.

Someone facing you
wants to speak but can't quite
articulate the bad news.

A roof set down miles away.
A tattered sleeve flapping
from a stripped branch.

Everything gone
gone the woman sobs
plucking at this this
and this remnant.

Hard to erase the scene
where the husband follows his wife upstairs,
she crying, haunted by an old love.

Murmuring soft words,
he unbuttons his shirt as they climb.

In a room at the end of the hall,
they strip and fall into bed.
The resolve—a glad ascending cry.

I wanted them to stay, sleep awhile.

Foolish how hopeful I was
knowing it couldn't end there,
the movie only three-quarters done.

Working in the garden today,
I let sorrow take root,

a chill in the soil I turn,
my hand no longer stroking your face,
the hours crumbling like loam.

Reprieves are brief.
Tonight a freeze could burn.

Dig, I say to myself, bury it.

FRACTURE

Above the Dardanelles, a sprinkle of stars
and farther on, Gallipoli.
From the third floor of the hotel
I looked down on a blue canopy
lit from below,
the men gathered there singing—
a harmony I wanted to join
praising what I could only feel,
the meaning inexplicable as love's tongue.

In the silent afterglow
I thought of you at home.
In less than a month you'd be gone,
the death I refused to foresee,
weeping instead over graves of strangers,
Muslims, Christians, buried side by side.

There seemed no resolution
for our quarrels
yet we could say the word *love*,
each time relearning the language,
wondering how it would translate,

wondering why
I'm still locked in the spell of that night,
the city's meanness hidden in shadows,
the bay broken by reflections
that even now slap me awake.

I want to lie in the forest
on hides stretched between poles,
my body left for birds to clean,
flesh flying off to a higher branch.

Or maybe in a mound
laden with obsessions,
a brimming chalice
rather than a begging cup.

In my hand, at last, the key
to the door that kept me knocking.

Part bone, part stain,
someone's lover lies
on the earthern floor
of a burial pit, the outline
of the torso flexed
in a familiar recline
once achingly relished.

Wayward flesh
restrained by virtuous bones.

When I was young
we scavenged cemetery plots,
moved vases and flowers
to the tombstones of kin.

I wake longing for one more chance
at the turn my story could have taken
before the part I regret ran out,
my hands, even now drawing on the hours,

some lightened, some smudged
by my touch, my play,
which at any given moment
could turn on you, could bury us both.

DRAWN INTO ARMS

Mars
a deep crimson
floating low.
An exhilaration of fireflies
    and stars
embossed on black.

Black
becoming to those of us
preparing to go out.

Late, warns the night,
time to leave.

No, not ready,
bound as I am
to the butterfly bush,
the zinnias, azaleas, and phlox,
    and you who cut
    and trim my life.

The darkened hedge, an altar
under a chalice of stars,
    particles and waves
    pouring around me—
a communion I want to share.

Will it hurt?
Will it rend
deeper than desire?

Desire kneels close
praying I won't let go.

This fruit, these glasses, these plates—
they talk to each other.

When your tongue slides over mine
I think I know everything about you—
scent and shape,

desire tilting toward us,
its color rounding out flesh,
flesh with its own
shimmering nuances

     ...fruits that set the mouth watering...

Touch soft-talks us into strokes
so subtle we hardly notice
how they run into shadows,
arrangements tumbling

     ...a paring knife in the corner...

Each time we set ourselves up
is a search for perfection,
the illusion of something tangible—

a hand caressing a hip,
a moon-washed quilt
slipping to the floor,
a voice calling out.

     They come to us laden,
     telling of the fields they have left behind,
     the rain that nourished them, the dawns.

There are changes with every light.

A loop of universe caught
by the swing of a telescope,
galaxies swirling out like words
when a rose becomes more
than scent or thorn,

the finger bleeding,
the mouth sucking its own
sweet fluidity, your tongue
covering mine, the body
shivering to recover its focus.

Beyond that I can't think,

can only hold on
to Joseph Cornell's
Starfish construction
which shifts with each shake
of the frame, the beach scene
never again repeating,

just as our footprints
disappear with the tide
that first brought us in.

So many unwitting escapes—
the universe handled blindly
until conjured
from a wheel of equations.

In Vermeer's painting
of *Woman Holding a Balance*
a flick of white on the scales
streaks through the darkness.

The pearls strewn across the table,
sublime little worlds
we imagine picked up by chance,

someone warm like you or I
holding them to the light
before trying them on,

their lustre increased
when they rest against flesh,
the throat pulsing,
the voice flying out.

I could make a wardrobe
with tufts of wool
caught on thistle and bracken.

Lost—the scraps
I might have woven whole cloth.

"Come watch," the man says,
shearing sheep
with the precision of long practice,
fleece, removed all of a piece,
rolled in a neat bundle.

I've been so clumsy
with people who've loved me.

Straddling a ewe,
the man props its head on his foot,
leans down with clippers,
each pass across the coat a caress.

His dogs, lying nearby,
tremble at every move—as I do,
loving the hands that have learned
to gentle the life beneath them.

STALKING

I could barely see,
but shot at what moved,
followed blood on the leaves
to the place the buck fell,
the body still warm,
eyes not yet glazed.

Kneeling down
I slit the throat
and pushed away
in case he kicked—
the way the dying do,
protesting to the last
regardless of pain.

Baby, my father used to say,
squeeze the trigger gentle-like.

Blood on the kitchen floor,
the smell of neat's-foot oil,
a clean stock.

I relish the flesh
of roasted venison,
its pungent taste
bursting on the tongue.

There isn't a bone
I wouldn't gnaw
to marrow, and suck.

Hungry, hungry—
remember that when I ease
up to you.

Admit it, we're drawn to the mysterious
like this geode opened after long darkness.

A rim of agate around amethyst—
clutch of daggers, flashy lights.

What a surprise to find
the basic compounds long-solidified.

Desire, envy, spite—aren't we all here?

Geodes smoldering in a river bank.
The most coveted disclosure—

a crevice opening on murderous thoughts
vitrified, the knife stilled before the plunge,
the bomb imploding into smoky quartz.

Soil and sand are fraught with minute crystals.

Forgetful of who we are,
we walk over ourselves every day.

FIRING CAN BE WILD

Once I was good with a gun,
held the stock firm
in the loll of my shoulder,
relished the feel of the kick,
the sure trajectory.

My aim hasn't changed,
but I tell myself I'm more watchful
in the same lush foolery.

Surprising, how one small bird
can scatter a reverie of leaves.

He takes two steps to her one
up the museum stairs.
Slow down, she murmurs
and moves closer
as they enter the gallery.

The girl in the painting stares
at them with parted lips,
her headdress a slash of blue,
the light across her face
a spray of crushed pearls.

Small hairs from the artist's brush
lie in half-tones of skin.

You know I have to leave,
he says without turning.
She circles his wrist with her fingers.

Gone.
The vacuum filled with a rush
of people she drifts behind.

Years into another life,
the story settles.

Under the darkening surface,
the moist hint of a tongue,
the surprise of desire.

RUNNING AWAY

You, cycling down a dirt road,
each rut an offense,
cattle with sorrowful eyes,
a dying orchard
in the field beyond.

You, dodging the day,
afraid it might lift you
on its horns, afraid
the night might break in

and find desire
wadded in your mouth,

an impassioned letter
trampled on the floor,

the words you memorized
sliding off with the light.

How many times have I lent myself
to a character devised by someone else,
the voice an aside
from my own true story.

Today I ran into my reflection in a mirror,
dislocation like that of a landscape
after the painter reassigns
verities of color and line.

A second look and I was back
to my original.

Say memory is a bruise
reminding us who we harmed,
who harmed us, and why
some felt so little of the blow.

Where does it hurt—where? we ask.
The child can't always say,
leaving us frantic
to know where to lay the salve.

It's not forgiveness I want,
it's the chance to revise
the roles I failed,
the never ending chance
to play the story of myself.

The road narrows to a countryside
I've traveled before.

Around a curve the same crumbled house,
lone chimney and jagged run of wall.

A place inhabited by weather and vista.

Say a window is open
and I'm willing to crawl through.

Once I climbed a cliff beside a waterfall,
roots and rock my ladder.
At the top I stripped and slid
into a pool.
Beyond boulders, water gave way
to a wild plunge.

And now you, my body awakened
from its long fast.
Sweet mornings, bells in the distance,
tongue, tongue, the moon, its light
dissolving into patterns
on the ceiling above the bed.

an indecent hour for those who don't mind
losing their lives in sleep.

The neighbor's dog nearly knocks me over
when I stoop to pick up the paper.

At least I'm loved
while others still dream.

Low in the sky, Venus fools again
with my heart. I stand in the dark,

half-bare, thinking of the one who died,
moon flooding the hours.

I almost drowned until you came along
and laid me down.

The dog wants to play. Go home,
I say, the night's not done.

WHAT IT COMES DOWN TO

A loud week
of yellow orange maroon
leaves and now this silence

this fear of someone
kicking through my remains

or the way it is after making love
me hanging on
as if my life depended on

whispers laughter bass & treble
the layers smoldering
in their own heat.

Each season the same surprise
how easily touch can bring me down.

Rain to slush to ice and snow,
one flake floating past
a silent other
    gone

moment trailing from moments
though the day seems long
while we're digging out

from the door
to wherever we might go
leaning on someone's arm

warm as fluffed birds, down
bit by bit preened
    loose drifting

the Milky Way sliding over the night
whether or not we watch
Jupiter brazening the dark,
Venus the dawn,

the lawn stained by a full moon,
the living by the dead,
wherever they are
    invisible

lines connecting the stars—
configurations we name
as if to bring them close.

as if we weren't worth spying on,
night taking charge with slitted eyes,

the world drowsing off,
lurching as it slows,
you and I pulled in separate ways.

Stay, I say, coverlet and pillow
flung to the floor, the ozone torn
where we break through,

Venus in the hammock of the new moon,
Jupiter leaning over.

One more pass at love before we free-float,
reckless, taking no notice,
a throng of regrets beckoning us back.

Behind us a deep sigh,
lights turning off.

Yesterday is overgrown
with briars and nettles,
a graveyard, broken names.

I try to coax the past into shape
but dreams dissipate,
today's gate
hanging on its one frangible hinge.

Show me a crimson climber
spilling over the rail
and I'll hum the day by.

Once I heard a woman
singing in a field,
her voice bell-like and true
as she bent to pluck
the blossoming bolls,
her hands bleeding
from wounds that had healed,
opened again, healed.

HAUNTED BY RUIN

"We play games until death comes to fetch us."
Kurt Schwitters

Who knows how far you wind
along the mountain trail
before the falls become memory,
now and then a clearing,
the sound of water—
or is it regret—cascading.

Each time you stand
drenched in spray,
a rainbow holding you tranced,
you forget the climb back
is more difficult
this year than last.

Rounding an overhang,
you're shocked
eye to eye with a buck.
Before you've had your fill,
he wheels, hooves scattering
rock, underbrush closing
over his flanks.

In the stillness,
the feral odor of galax
rouses that deep fear,
the heaviness you sense
bearing down too fast,
your erratic heart
scrambling upslope.

You stop to rest
on the root-riddled path
that has drawn you up
as often as let you down.
The sun leaves ash, the moon
splits between clouds
stars ticking on and off.
You hardly notice
how weather picks you to shreds.

Hours, days, years
pass in this wilderness.
You begin to sing out
the bell-tones of sorrel,
bluets, lobelia, trillium.
The way it is at night
when a child kneels for prayers,
calling all the names he loves
before the lights switch off.

by its gravity, bloody and green
in the savageness of change—

flowering camellias scorched by last night's ice,
a child carried screaming from a shelled house,
fragmented bodies identified by shreds of cloth
pulled from the line that morning and ironed.

I've said it before—whenever I hold your face
and look at you straight, I'm afraid of time so sweet.

Yet, I want you to tell me again
how true for the moment you are,
the tongue tasting my body no lie,
no powder burns on the hands gentling my fears.

I pocket a shard or two from scattered slabs,
pieces of a frieze washed with faint color
once spectacular, even gaudy,

the statues bleached as we are at night
strafed by the moon.

Sometimes I reach over and touch
to find if you're still flesh and whole,
no taint of history breaking in
to find us asleep, mouths open, legs spread.

Our wars are over, love, our weapons buried
where we long since agreed not to go.

Nothing to excess engraved on a wall
yet we were at our best
before exposure brought us down,
all that we were never fully retrieved,

the bronze hairs on your chest,
my hair spilled across your face.

Day ransacks the room and leaves
us breeding shadows.

...the hall fallen in decay, no talking spring,
the stream dry that had so much to say

Relics, colonnades, pedestals, strewn
between the mountain's knees.

A laurel crooks up from beneath a wall,
and splits the obdurate stone—

fragments I covet. *Drop it,*
the guard commands but I can't
leave the broken past alone, want
to enshrine it like something holy,
saving me.

An unexpected opening of three orchids on a plant
that hasn't bloomed in years, a spread of white fans,
the spurred lip stained with yellow as is the cup

no bee drinks from in the room's conditioned atmosphere,
my life too in its second wind waiting for the thrust
of some random hunger, unlikely to arrive

as a trilobite to swim from stone, or for bubbles
in this crystal ball I hold to explode as they once did
when I dove, rising with them to the surface

in a silvery school of air, the sort of glitter that flashes
roadside as we drive by at 70 mph, leaving behind a whole
landscape—the aunt who each day put the house to bed,

her hand sliding across the burnished grain
of a grandfather clock, late light running down the minutes
leaving chimes for me to tend until the hour

the pendulum suspends its swing, until the day
no horizon blocks passage into changing clouds that I,
as a child lying on sweetgrass, watch without fear.

These are the scales we first practiced:
moist nights, leaves whispering to rain,
the pulse's quickening hum—lost

as the porcelain cup I found
on a mossy ledge in the woods,
the spring below murmuring over watercress.

And I knelt down as we all must do
if we're to tongue the stream teasing past
resonant with stone, silt, grass,
and excrement
often so diluted we're unaware

of the dark spill,
the true/false story of our lives,
and the voices that inhabit us, pouring
from room to over-flowing room,
the aria playing itself out.

RESURRECTION SITES

When elephants come across skeletons of their dead
they stroke the length and width of bones
as if transfiguring them to a whole.

I don't know what's become of you.

Below the castle in Prague, streets twist
sternly dark, the long row of houses huddled
like frightened children, windows closed,

an occasional light in a room inhabited by someone
reading to another, a pot of tea on a table between chairs,
the history of fear subsumed by what's become of them.

Leave them where they are, you said at Melos
as I dug up bits of pottery with my nails,
the guide droning on.

In an attic I found a locket with a twine of hair.
Open and close, open, close on a conjured past
more lucid than the real and all that paled.

What's become of you I don't know.

I pocket what I can and keep it
fingered to a shine.

Remember the scene in the movie
where the strung-out vet
loses a game of Russian roulette?
After the funeral back home,
friends gather around a table, glum,
silent, waiting for coffee and beer.

Someone starts humming *God Bless America*
and they all join in, shaky and off-key.
I'm an easy weep for those endings,
can forget for a time the horror done.

Once in a motel I put my ear to the wall
and listened to the adjacent room.
Crying. A crash. Curses and moans.
Come to bed, you cajoled (soft touch, safe move),

but I wanted a fragment of that other life,
a reminder of the damaged years, the harm
still lingering on our lips, the taste for blood
that can't be kissed away.

THE DEAD

The dead sift through us
without flesh, bone, hair,
or whatever else the stars concoct
for us to touch.

Reaching for the velvet muzzle
of a horse, their hands pass on through
never feeling the warm breath in their palms.

Try catching wind as it runs over wheat
leaving it in shocked repose.

Cruel—to see the one you love
and realize neither tongue nor limb,
desire an unattached shadow.

Dashing without thought against the day,
we complain at the slightest wound.
The dead drift by longing for a bruise.

We meet despite the odds, your hands
scribbling intricate equations across my flesh.

I trace your back, you move my body.

In the aftermath we lie fitful,
falling into dreams the other won't admit,

some nightmares so bloody
we're afraid they might wake.

It's been a difficult landing.
We could easily have drifted away.

Denying emptiness, I fill in outlines:
Orion and The Bear—warrior and beast
forever at our heels.

No use trying to connect heaven,
lines trail off, stars pile one over another,
atom, quark, neutrino, chance stumbling in.

Like night-eyes in a forest,
tomorrow glimmers
without a discernible body.

I zoom in on the scattering herd.
Maybe it's the early hour, or luck, or both—
the guide tells us it's the first time
she's seen as many reindeer on the plateau.

A stag stops for a moment on the ridge,
his antlers crazing the broody sky.

Nuzzling down to lichen and sedge,
his soft mouth pushes snow aside,
warm breath melting the patches of ice.

In the hard light, water glistens,
reflections shunted this way, that.

At this altitude I'm giddy enough
to kneel at a glacial stream. *Don't drink!*
Too late—my cupped hands
have already dropped from my face.

There's an acid twist
to the sweet run-offs I've savored
with little thought of where they wind.

And now I ask you to hold still.
It's all I can do to keep your image sharp.
Here, where sustenance barely rides
the permafrost, I want to reach out
and pull you in—close as we are to the edge.

If music refused Bach
he prayed his sins undone,
not like us dissonant ones
quick to trade earth and stars
for a wish come true.

His notes still swell
the clouds that float our way.
A banner reading PARADISE
trails the deluge,
the name itself musical,
casting its spell
on the world below.

I wonder what word was used
long ago when someone first thought
to bury the dead.
Speech was likely broken-toned,
the unknown left unsaid.

It's doubtful any were aware
how shade and echo amplified
the voice, the tree, or the bodies
they laid in the ground.
Yet someone threw
cornflowers, hyacinths, yarrow,
into Stone Age graves,
an act that moved in counterpoint
to scales the double helix plays.

Bach confessing his fugue
in an empty church.

Walk around St. Catherine's Hill
and you'll see the sides ribbed
with reminders of an Iron Age fort,
the slopes not so far away as they seem
from ducks and geese
riffling the meadow streams.

It's possible to recall a whole life
from remains, a ship from nailheads
and imprints, those who sailed
showing up like refugees
worn from centuries of storm.

High on a ledge
of Winchester Cathedral,
the bones of Canute and his queen
lie jumbled in a casket.
An intimate disorder.

One text of the Bible
opens on an unfinished page
of roughed-in figures the eye fills
with colors of its own choosing.
Words are gold illuminating the hours.

Mead spilled from lip into song
from this silver flagon traded across water.

In late afternoon when shadows
overflow, our communion with the past
breaking the day, you can almost believe
walls still ring the mound,

reflections dropping into a pool
where they shatter
in the wake of a black swan
before rushing back whole.

to my boat   drifting
  smaller smaller
the tether I held   trailing
loose   tenuous   shadow
of spruce   strung across water
we dive into   depths
not yet plumbed   shapes
too dark to name
or invoke remembrance   who
will lift us   breathe into us
to swim again
   floundering
if not in these waters   others
as we clutch anything afloat
a disturbance of ripples
   flattening out
a pileated woodpecker's
raucous goodbye   passing over
   all all
meditations
   tangled on the wharf
worthless I decide
back-stroking across the lake.

You've seen a child stop at play
to stare, as through a fog,
at some barely outlined form
not fleshed enough to recognize.

In time you'll come to understand
where your life changed and why.

Like traces of ancient earthworks—
ramparts, barrows, grids
you walk over and by, unaware—
the past becomes more penetrable
viewed from afar, relics
washed out here and there, found,
all the windswept acres resonant.

Before entering, look down
a crumbling nave to the choir,
colors from the clerestory
playing the air of all you believe,
want to believe.

Never mind the dank remainders
of the dead who fail to resurrect.

And when bells begin to chime,
never mind the small ghost
left drifting. At night it will wander
home to your arms, and when it cries
you will croon *hush hush*,
singing the runes heard
countless times, countless ways.

Dreams stay busy all night
changing into this costume or that.
Hold me, a lover dares, but the fickle scenes
dump us from bed to unmade bed.

Good morning, I'm able to say—
the day's felt hammer
striking a taut wire.

Dancing around the sphere
of a bar-room floor,
I press as close to you as I can,
your breath in my hair.

Time for bed, you whisper,
and I shiver for the one who'll wake
to find the other not there,

the unfinished script improvising
another day into night,
stars again making an entrance.

That moment of suspense—
a threshold we linger on
before we're whirled out
beyond control, beyond caring.

LEAVING THE WORLD
WE'VE LOVED SPEECHLESS

The letter A is a tent that held us for a while.
Now we're restless to leave the alphabet
and ride off into numbers.

But numbers can't divine
the luminous grove we could happen upon,
you and I stretched on the same sliver of time,
its stream winding down into fragrance,
our shadows now plaited, now loose.

In the warm intersection of sex and love,
the mouth puckers as soon as we're born,
starved no matter how often and deep
we push into someone else.

Numbers tell how we come and go
yet fail to fathom a woman's grief
as she tosses on a bed she can't fill.

The purity of numbers deceives us
into thinking they're true,
could never be found in a stranger's arms.

Numbers wasted on wars
rough up the contours of history,
the landscape defined by a blast of white,
the grass we greened gone, the mare
no longer nuzzling the child's palm.

Maybe Voyager, floating in its frigid sea of stars,
will land and voices once more disembark.
Absurd to think our slow-motion scatter of dust
is the beginning and end of words
announcing we've come, we've gone.

From the edge of the woods to the oak,
the pear tree, and now the roof,
the owl is all over us tonight,
and farther the stars
tossing us out in the cold.

From our warren of a bed, it's easy to forget
the agnostic bones hidden in believable flesh
our fingers insist on exploring,

the ranting of hands a braille, touch
trying to spell more than is there
each time we approach the verbs of love.

When we climbed the hill to Cueva de la Pileta,
a sputtering lamp led to animals, grids,
hands, outlined on stone, the passage mute
except for our chatter.

To save ourselves from erasure,
we change the subject to an answerable code,
a word or gesture that allows us
into the body of all we live,

labyrinths sometimes losing us,
sometimes leading us into a sanctum,
the ones we've loved rising from their sleep,
not whole, but an aura
we wrap ourselves in when weathers turn.

Twice as a child I was shaken out of myself.
A squall of light blew over and through me,
the surrounding world shimmering alive,
all things equal—leaf, house, bird—
and I was touched as no one, nothing,
has touched me since, casting ever after
for repeat of that call.